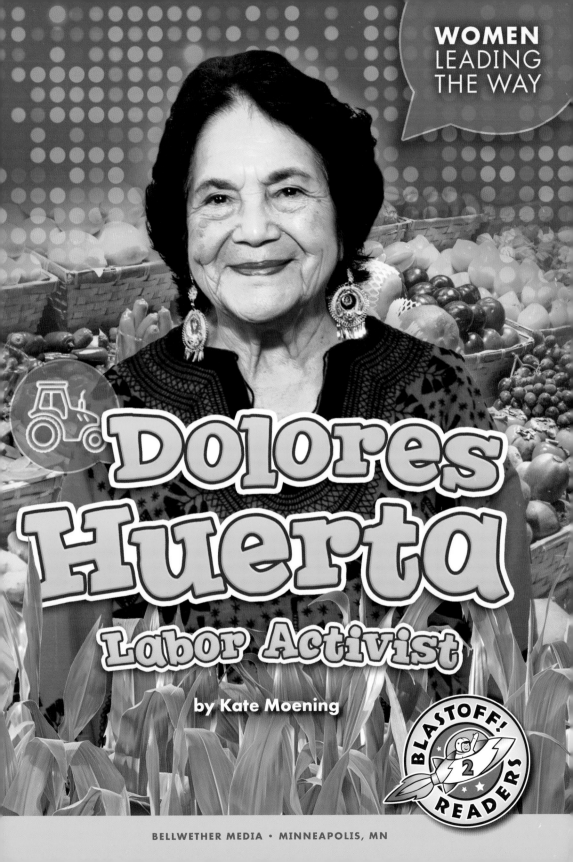

WOMEN
LEADING
THE WAY

# Dolores Huerta
## Labor Activist

by Kate Moening

BLASTOFF!
2
READERS

BELLWETHER MEDIA • MINNEAPOLIS, MN

Note to Librarians, Teachers, and Parents:

**Blastoff! Readers** are carefully developed by literacy experts and combine standards-based content with developmentally appropriate text.

**Level 1** provides the most support through repetition of high-frequency words, light text, predictable sentence patterns, and strong visual support.

**Level 2** offers early readers a bit more challenge through varied simple sentences, increased text load, and less repetition of high-frequency words.

**Level 3** advances early-fluent readers toward fluency through increased text and concept load, less reliance on visuals, longer sentences, and more literary language.

**Level 4** builds reading stamina by providing more text per page, increased use of punctuation, greater variation in sentence patterns, and increasingly challenging vocabulary.

**Level 5** encourages children to move from "learning to read" to "reading to learn" by providing even more text, varied writing styles, and less familiar topics.

Whichever book is right for your reader, Blastoff! Readers are the perfect books to build confidence and encourage a love of reading that will last a lifetime!

This edition first published in 2020 by Bellwether Media, Inc.

No part of this publication may be reproduced in whole or in part without written permission of the publisher. For information regarding permission, write to Bellwether Media, Inc., Attention: Permissions Department, 6012 Blue Circle Drive, Minnetonka, MN 55343.

Library of Congress Cataloging-in-Publication Data

Names: Moening, Kate, author.
Title: Dolores Huerta : Labor Activist / by Kate Moening.
Description: Minneapolis, MN : Bellwether Media, Inc., 2020. | Series: Blastoff! Readers: Women Leading the Way | Includes bibliographical references and index.
Identifiers: LCCN 2018053538 (print) | LCCN 2018054173 (ebook) | ISBN 9781618916716 (ebook) | ISBN 9781644870990 (hardcover : alk. paper) | ISBN 9781618917225 (pbk. : alk. paper)
Subjects: LCSH: Huerta, Dolores, 1930–Juvenile literature. | Women labor leaders–United States–Biography–Juvenile literature. | Mexican American women labor union members–Biography–Juvenile literature.
Classification: LCC HD6509.H84 (ebook) | LCC HD6509.H84 M64 2020 (print) | DDC 331.4/7813092 [B] –dc23
LC record available at https://lccn.loc.gov/2018053538

Editor: Al Albertson     Designer: Andrea Schneider

Printed in the United States of America, North Mankato, MN.

# Table of **Contents**

# Who Is Dolores Huerta?

Dolores Huerta is an **activist**. She fights for **migrant farmers** and women.

She helped start the **United Farm Workers of America**!

**United Farm Workers of America members**

"WE MUST USE OUR LIVES TO **MAKE THE WORLD A BETTER PLACE TO LIVE**, NOT JUST TO ACQUIRE THINGS."

Dolores was born in New Mexico. There her dad fought for **unions**. Then her parents **divorced**.

She moved to California
with her mom and brothers.

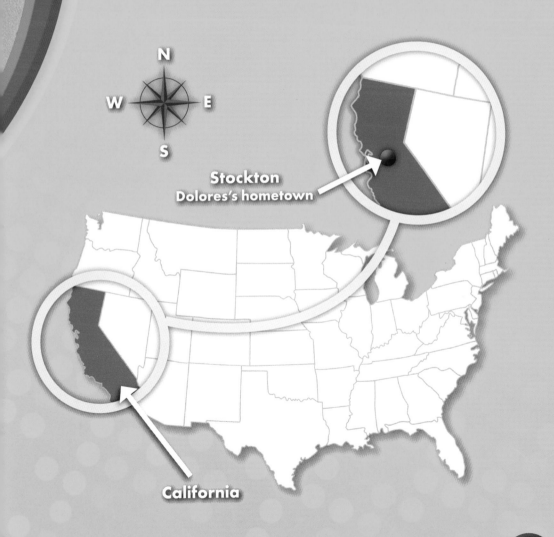

N

W    E

S

Stockton
Dolores's hometown

California

Most of their neighbors in California were **immigrants** and farmers. Dolores's mom was a leader in their community.

# Dolores Huerta Profile

**Birthday:** April 10, 1930

**Hometown:** Stockton, California

**Industry:** community organizing

**Education:**
- teaching degree (University of Pacific's Delta College)

**Influences and Heroes:**
- Alicia Chavez (mother)
- Juan Fernandez (father)
- Fred Ross (labor activist)

She taught Dolores to speak her mind. Young Dolores also loved Girl Scouts.

Dolores became a teacher. Many of her students' families were farmers. But **growers** paid them little money.

Dolores knew this was wrong. She became an activist!

farmers working for a lettuce grower

10

DON'T BUY GRAPES

Votes on meetings

11

# Changing the World

Dolores with Cesar Chavez

Dolores joined a group that helped Mexican-American families. She met another activist named Cesar Chavez.

Dolores and Cesar both wanted to help the farmers.

13

Dolores and Cesar planned a **boycott** and a **strike**. Dolores shouted "*Si se puede!*" In Spanish it means, "Yes, we can!"

Dolores's activism worked! The growers paid the farmers more.

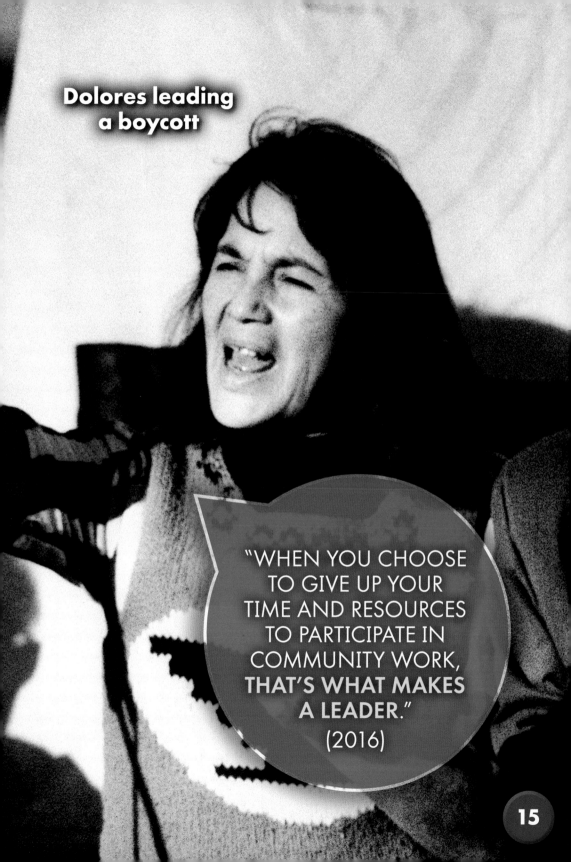

Dolores leading a boycott

"WHEN YOU CHOOSE TO GIVE UP YOUR TIME AND RESOURCES TO PARTICIPATE IN COMMUNITY WORK, THAT'S WHAT MAKES A LEADER." (2016)

Dolores as a young activist

Being a woman and a leader was hard. Daycare helped Dolores care for her 11 children.

Women leaders were not always respected, either. Cesar got the **credit**. Dolores learned to stand up for herself!

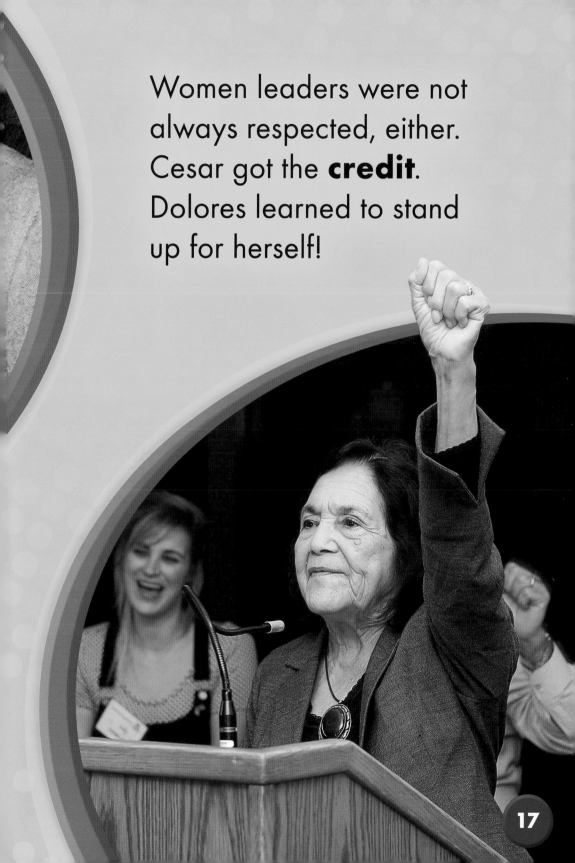

# Dolores's Future

Dolores has won many **awards**.
But her work is not done!

# Dolores Huerta Timeline

**1955**  Dolores leaves teaching to work in community organizing

**1962**  Dolores and Cesar Chavez form what is now the United Farm Workers of America to help pass laws that keep farm workers safe

**1965**  Dolores helps organize a grape boycott to make sure farm workers are treated fairly

**1975**  Dolores helps pass a law that gives California farm workers power to disagree with growers

**2002**  Dolores creates the Dolores Huerta Foundation to help community groups

She still speaks about workers' and women's **rights**.

Dolores wants people to use their voices for change. She makes sure people vote.

Dolores wants people to know they have power!

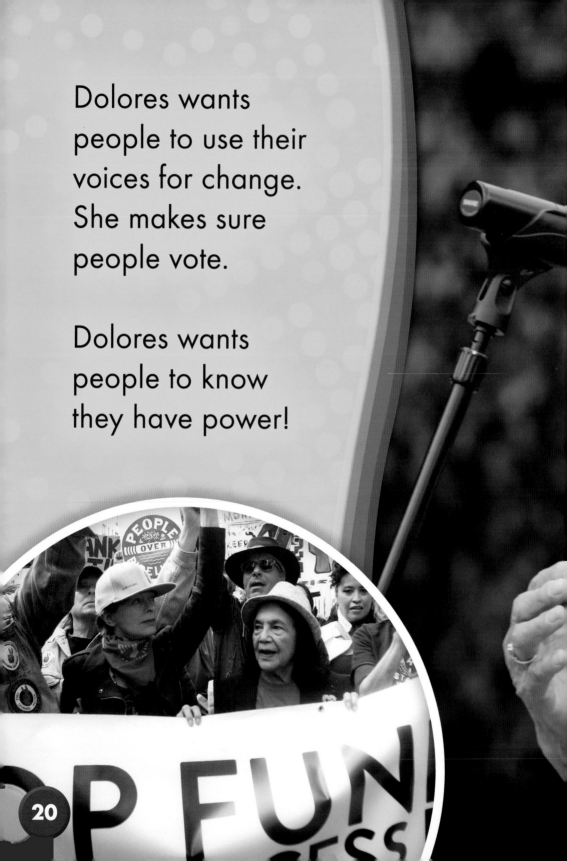

"YOU ALREADY HAVE THE POWER... WE JUST NEED TO COME TOGETHER AND WORK TO MAKE CHANGE." (2018)

# Glossary

**activist**—a person who believes in taking action to make changes in laws or society

**awards**—rewards or prizes that are given for a job well done

**boycott**—an event in which people refuse to buy or do something; activists often use boycotts to make change happen.

**credit**—praise or attention for making something happen

**divorced**—separated and stopped being married

**growers**—people who grow large amounts of a plant or crop to sell; growers often hire farmers to take care of the crops.

**immigrants**—people who leave one country to live in another

**migrant farmers**—workers who move around to where there are good crops to farm

**rights**—things that every person should be allowed to have, get, or do

**strike**—a time when workers refuse to work until their needs are met

**unions**—organized groups of workers formed to protect their rights

**United Farm Workers of America**—a group that fights for farmers' rights, such as good conditions and fair pay

# To Learn More

## AT THE LIBRARY

Barghoorn, Linda. *Dolores Huerta: Advocate for Women and Workers*. New York, N.Y.: Crabtree Publishing Company, 2017.

Moening, Kate. *Malala Yousafzai: Education Activist*. Minneapolis, Minn.: Bellwether Media, 2020.

Penguin Random House LLC. *The Little Book of Little Activists*. New York, N.Y.: Viking, 2017.

## ON THE WEB

**FACTSURFER**

Factsurfer.com gives you a safe, fun way to find more information.

1. Go to www.factsurfer.com.

2. Enter "Dolores Huerta" into the search box and click 🔍.

3. Select your book cover to see a list of related web sites.

# Index